A Bereavec

By Steve Younis

Printed in the United States of America by CreateSpace.com

Second Printing: February 2011

ISBN 1450596916
EAN-13 9781450596916

Contents

This book,
like everything else in my life,
is dedicated to my wife,
Sonia.

Also for my angels in heaven,
Jasmine and Sophie.

Introduction

If you are reading this, then there is a high probability that, like me, you are a father who has lost a child. In my case, two children. My only two children. While I have no children living in my house, I am still a father.

It is an odd thing being a father but having no children to be a father to. It is a hollow feeling, but one that remains with you forever.

My wife Sonia and I were married in July 1994. In 2003, after nine years of marriage we finally fell pregnant. It was our 5th attempt at IVF, having tried unsuccessfully to fall pregnant for many years previous. We were elated.

The pregnancy seemed to be going well. No morning sickness, gaining weight nicely. Like most young couples we just thought everything would go as planned. On July 24, 2003, one day after our ninth wedding anniversary, our lives changed forever. Twenty weeks into the pregnancy, a mere thirty minutes after having visited the Obstetrician where everything seemed fine, in the bathroom of our home, our first child, a girl, came into the world. It was the most harrowing experience of my life. The memory of that day still haunts me.

Jasmine, our daughter, was alive for a few minutes. But was too premature to survive. As I rode in the ambulance to the hospital, I could barely fathom what had happened. I was numb, but attempted to remain strong for my wife.

The hospital stay, the grieving family and friends, the funeral, the next six months are all a blur in my memory.

Facing major dates such as Christmas, Birthdays, Anniversaries, suddenly becomes a trauma that you never envisioned you would ever associate with those occasions. And just after Sonia and I faced our first Christmas in this bleak new world, we discovered that we had fallen pregnant naturally.

This second pregnancy was a rollercoaster ride. While we wanted to be happy, thinking naively that a natural pregnancy was a "sign", we were frightened sick of having the same thing happen twice. We remained sane only by the reassurance that we were now considered a high-risk pregnancy and would therefore be monitored more closely by expert doctors and professors.

We passed the dreaded twenty-week gestation period, where the first pregnancy had failed. We hoped beyond hope that this milestone was a positive omen.

Nevertheless, on July 11, 2004, fourteen weeks premature, (not one year since the birth and death of Jasmine), our second daughter, Sophie was born in the hospital where she survived for three days. On July 14 she passed away, having fought valiantly to remain with us. During those three days our family and close friends were able to meet Sophie. Something nobody was able to do with Jasmine. This made the funeral a more sorrowful experience for the extended family, with Sophie seeming more real to everyone else who never had the chance to meet Jasmine.

Strangely enough, Sophie's funeral for me was not as difficult as Jasmine's had been. After all I had been through it before. I knew what to expect. How small the coffin would be. I understood what was expected of me. What my responsibilities were.

You will no doubt have heard that men and women grieve differently. It is true mostly. As men, society tells us that we are not supposed to cry. That we have to be the "strong one". The rock. Society has it wrong. I am not ashamed to say I cried. Many times. What kind of person would I be if I was not devastated by the death of my own children?

However men do tend to grieve differently to women. We generally find it easier to deal with our emotions by remaining active. We work through our emotions internally, in our own heads, while our hands are keeping busy. As husbands we generally want to be able to think we can fix what needs fixing, making right that which is wrong. But when your child dies you feel useless. How can you possibly set things right when everything has gone so utterly wrong? It is out of your hands.

As a creative person, being a graphic designer by profession and playing the guitar as a hobby, I poured my feelings into writing poems and songs. I even painted a wall mural of two cherubs in our stairwell as a way of bringing my girls into our home.

Family and friends seem to focus on the mother. After all she is the one lying in the hospital bed, she is the one who gave birth. To an extent I was okay with all that. I felt I was managing okay. The last thing I wanted to do was take away any of the support that was being directed towards my wife. She desperately needed the love and support that family and friends were giving her.

However a small part of me felt left out. Most people upon visiting us would ask, "How's Sonia?" It was usually an after thought when they remembered to ask, "Oh yeah, how are you doing? Are you okay?"

Generally I have found that most people have no idea what to say when they see you, especially when seeing you for the first time since the loss of your baby. I have had well-meaning people say things like "You're both still young, you'll have other children", I would look at them and politely nod or shrug my shoulders, preferring not to say anything, because my mind was yelling, "Why? Are any of your children any less precious to you than the others? Even if I do have other children, they'll never replace the ones I've lost!" They mean well, they don't realise that some of the things they say are actually hurtful or naive. But people feel the need to say something, when personally I was just appreciative that they cared enough to visit Sonia and I. No words could console us. Their presence alone was enough.

As the father, the man, I found I was also automatically required to handle the clerical side of the death of my child. Hospital paperwork, funeral arrangements, documents needing to be signed. How do you prepare yourself to deal with Birth Certificates and Death Certificates at the same time? I found myself trying to shelter my wife from having to deal with things like explaining to Medicare why we needed to remove our daughter's name from our account and have new cards re-issued again.

I have heard of couples who, having experienced the death of a child, found themselves unable to continue on with their relationship. I could not imagine anything like this ever happening to Sonia and I. The experience of losing our girls has strengthened our relationship, brought us closer. We relied on each other throughout it all. We spoke constantly about how we felt. We continue to speak about our girls. We know we are changed people, but we are mostly comfortable with who we are.

My wife used to be much more outspoken. She was school captain of her high school. I on the other hand used to be quite reserved. After everything that has happened, my wife sometimes feels incapable of speaking in front of people. She is a lot more emotional than she used to be, less confident. My experiences brought forth an inner resolve I never knew I had.

While years have passed since we lost Jasmine and Sophie, and the pain of their loss does lessen over time, I know it will never fully go away, and I would not want it to.

A Bereaved Father

Special occasions like Christmas, Easter, Birthdays, Anniversaries, Mothers Day and Fathers Day can be difficult. I don't personally think ahead too far, but my wife does, and I know in her mind she builds dark clouds around these up-coming occasions, dreading what will happen, how she will cope. Over the years we have discovered that the dread leading up to these days is almost always far worse than the actual day itself. You just manage somehow. You find the strength and discover that it was not as bad as you had built it up to be.

Family and friends, having felt your loss with you, will get on with their lives a lot quicker. You may find yourself resenting them for it. It is easy to think that everyone around you has forgotten your lost child or children. Nobody seems to talk about them anymore. I have found that most people are worried that speaking about your child will upset you, so they think things are best left alone. You know what? We do get upset, but that is okay. We get upset because our babies have died, not because you mention their names. Just the fact that someone remembers to acknowledge that your child was real makes it all worthwhile.

I found attending the SIDS and Kids support groups very beneficial. I was able to talk about my feelings of loss, of broken dreams and shattered plans, and look across the room and see nodding faces that totally understood where I was coming from, rather than blank stares from friends who meant well but could never truly appreciate what we had been through.

Sonia and I have no other children. Our family photos from now on will always be missing two people.

My experience may be similar to your own. It may be totally different. But if you have lost a child, then we are part of the same club that nobody ever wants to join, but a club you have nevertheless become a life member of.

It's not easy. It's not supposed to be. But I have found, whether you are a man or a woman, being open about your feelings, communicating with your partner, your family, your friends, and other grieving parents can really help.

It's not easy... but it's not impossible.

The pages that follow are filled with my thoughts and experiences on a range of topics associated with being a bereaved father. While I have no formal training as a grief counselor or as a psychiatrist, I am unfortunately an "expert" in the area of being a bereaved father. I live it 24/7 365 days a year. Hopefully by sharing my personal experiences you (whether you be a bereaved father or mother) will be able to identify some similarities with your own experiences, and find some solace in knowing that you are not going crazy, you are not abnormal, and you are not alone.

Being a Bereaved Father

If you are a bereaved parent your story will be different to mine, and different to every other bereaved parent's story. Yet there are also many similarities. Similarities that unite us in a way that is both reassuring as well as upsetting.

While I have no other children, your family may be made up of children born and raised before or after the baby you lost. You may have had fewer or more losses than my own. Your loss may have been due to miscarriage, premature birth, stillbirth, termination, SIDS or other factors. Whatever the case may be, being the father of child who has died is not something easy to deal with.

Being a bereaved father was not something I had ever considered, nor was it something anyone had ever discussed with me. It just never entered my mind.

When my wife finally became pregnant, nobody discussed the possibility that the pregnancy would be anything else other than successful. There were no classes or literature that I know of that was given to us that went anywhere near the topic. Everything focused on a positive outcome.

It is easy to look back at that time and that fact with a cynical eye and be critical of the "system" for not preparing us better. But when you think about it logically, I cannot imagine how my wife and I would have reacted at the time if someone came up to us with a "doom and gloom" warning about the possibility that our baby might die.

Sure, I now know that babies do die. It's a fact. However most do not. (It is generally estimated that one in four pregnancies fail). So it only stands to reason that the normal (and humane) practice is to approach pregnancy preparation from the positive point of view that it will be successful and you will have a healthy baby that will grow up into a child and beyond.

Even if there had been some kind of educational warning, what father in his right mind would entertain the thought that it might happen to his child? As I said before, it never entered my mind.

Nevertheless, I am a bereaved father. But what does that mean? What does "bereaved" actually mean?

By definition, "Bereavement" is an objective state of having 'lost' someone significant.

Being a bereaved father is not something I ever considered, nor something I wanted to be. However, it is now who I am. In many ways it defines me. Like it or not, it is now part of my identity.

Being a bereaved father is complicated. It changes your life... forever. Strangely enough not all those changes are negative ones.

Grief

When my daughters died I went through a myriad of different emotions: Sadness, Despair, Anger, Confusion, Shock, Disbelief, Guilt, Loneliness, and Anxiety.

A million and one questions raced through my mind.

"How could this happen to us?"

"Why did this happen to us?"

"What do I do now?"

"Will Sonia be okay?"

"What do I tell people?"

"Why did God allow this to happen?"

"Could I have done something differently?"

"How do we survive this?"

I remember that one of the stranger questions to enter my mind was regarding the name of our baby. We had always loved the name "Jasmine". At the time it was really the only girl's name my wife and I had totally agreed on. It was a name we both loved, and one nobody else in our immediate family and friends had used. When our first daughter died, I remember thinking, "Do we use the name we picked? Should we name her Jasmine?" I just wasn't sure whether we should use the name we liked so much for a baby who would never get to hear us say it to her. Maybe that seems odd to you, but maybe you know exactly what I'm talking about. Looking back now, I'm glad we did call her by the name we had always intended to use. It just seems right.

As men we are conditioned by society, the way we are brought up, by our family and friends. We hear phrases like, "Real men don't cry". We are conditioned to believe that we have to be "the strong one", the rock and foundation of our family. The provider and protector.

These ideals bounce around in your head after your baby has died. They clash with the overwhelming emotions you are feeling.

I cried my eyes out. I sobbed so hard it scared me. I felt like I was going to fall apart. I felt lost. Nothing made sense. The world had been turned upside down and it was all I could do to hold on and stay on my feet.

I get angry now when I hear people say, "Real men don't cry". That is so much BS it makes me sick. How could I not cry? My baby, my own flesh and blood, the life I had helped to create, was dead!

Even months and years later, when talking about Jasmine and Sophie, I can be drawn to tears. There is nothing wrong with that. Not crying is easy. Being able to face your emotions as a father who has lost a child takes real strength.

Grief is a powerful thing. It really knocks you about. It is hard to find your bearings. It is difficult to know what is the right thing to do, both for you and your wife. It hampers the decision making process. It changes you both physically and emotionally. It manifests in different ways for different people.

But how do you deal with grief?

The one thing I do know: There is no right or wrong way to deal with grief.

You need to do what is right for you. Oh people will give you all sorts of advice on what you should do, how long it should take, what is proper and what is not. Listen to them, only because someone might suggest something that appeals to you. But at the end of the day, do what works for YOU.

There is no right or wrong way to grieve. Even between father and mother there will be differences. Big differences.

In my opinion the two most important things to know are:

A) You need to do what is right for you.

B) Men and women often grieve differently.

The Early Days

For me, through losing both my daughters, one of the strongest emotions I had was the need to make sure my wife was okay. That "Protector" instinct was very strong for me.

Jasmine, our first daughter, was born when my wife (at twenty weeks gestation) went to the bathroom. During her pregnancy with Sophie I would not allow her to go to the bathroom without me. It haunted me to think what might have happened if I had not been there when Jasmine was born. It made me sick to think of how Sonia would have coped in that situation alone. As it was it was the worst day of our lives, and we were there for each other. If she had been alone... I shudder at the idea of even trying to finish that thought.

During the turmoil it is easy for the husband to almost become the forgotten victim. The focus is on the mother. She is the one that has actually given birth. She is lying in the hospital bed. As the mobile and non-bed-ridden party the task falls to you to be the messenger, courier, spokesperson, organiser, and anything else that is required during the immediate aftermath.

This can be both a blessing and a burden. I found that I felt so helpless and useless at times. It was killing me to think that nothing I could do would make things better. It was out of my control. I was freewheeling and lost.

Having something constructive to do was at least something I could hold on to. It kept my mind busy, focused. Even if it was just something as mundane as having to go to the cupboard and grab her slippers, it was at least something tangible that I could do. Something constructive and helpful. Something sane.

But at times, quiet times when things had calmed down, I felt alone. Left out. Forgotten. The people that came and went, be they nurses or doctors, family or friends, usually forgot to ask me if I was okay or simply assumed I was fine. Those that did get around to asking about my well-being tended to do so as an afterthought, long after they had exhausted conversation about everything else that had gone on.

Don't get me wrong. I do not begrudge my wife one ounce of the care and attention she was given. While I would have given my right arm to make things right for her, I don't know if I would have coped if the roles were reversed. I will never fully understand what she went through. I am in awe of her.

One thing people do not seem to understand or think about when a baby dies during or after the mother gives birth is the fact that she still goes through all the hormonal and physical aspects of being a new mother. Dealing with lactation (the secretion of milk for the process of breastfeeding) seemed a cruel joke that I didn't feel prepared for. Thankfully Sonia's mother and my own mother stepped in with advice and aid to help Sonia in this area.

I remember in the days after Sophie was born, and Sonia was still in the Maternity Ward of the hospital, we were distraught about Sophie's condition and extremely emotional about her tenuous hold on life. It was hard being in the Maternity Ward, hearing all the other babies, in the rooms with their mothers, with their family and friends all cheerful and loud, while our baby was fighting a losing battle in the Neonatal Intensive Care unit. It was even harder when one of the nurses whose job it was to give assistance on the whole breastfeeding thing, obviously unaware of our situation, walked into Sonia's room and looked around with a quizzical look on her face and asked, "Where's your baby?" I can tell you she beat a hasty retreat with a look of sheer embarrassment on her face once I told her where Sophie was. I felt kind of sorry for the nurse, but at the same time was miffed at needing to explain the situation to someone who should have been better informed.

A fellow bereaved mother once told me that at the hospital she was staying in they had a practice of posting a butterfly sticker on the door to the room of a mother whose baby had died, as an indicator to the nursing staff. This struck me as a wonderful way of ensuring that people who needed to know about the plight of the family within knew the situation and were well informed, while everyone else passing by would be none the wiser and the family could remain sheltered from the rest of the world.

One of the hardest things I had to deal with early on was the role of messenger and spokesperson. Having to ring my family and my wife's family to let them know what had happened was numbing. Facing them when they arrived at the hospital was gut wrenching. Just when I thought I had managed to pull together some semblance of balance, confronting my family and seeing the pain on their faces for me, just blew open the floodgates. Seeing the anguish on the faces of my father and brother hit me hardest.

I had grown up seeing my father as the archetypal man. Strong, rugged, and hard working. A man who had started with little, but who had managed to build a life for himself and his family by working his fingers to the bone. A man of unlimited generosity, but one who never cried. He hadn't even cried at his mother's funeral. Yet here he was, devastated for me, and the loss of his granddaughter.

The role of spokesperson also involved paper work. The birth and death of a baby necessitate the filling out of forms. Birth certificates, death certificates, medical forms and other clerical documents needed to be filled out. Paperwork is not the easiest thing to deal with at the best of times, let alone at such a difficult time, but once again it gave me something to do. Something constructive and tangible.

However for me the need to "keep busy" was far out weighed by the need to be there for my wife. I felt bad when "responsibilities" took me away from her side. Her need to have me by her side was palpable. I felt like I was her security blanket. While I wasn't necessarily serving any constructive purpose standing by her bedside, it was nevertheless where she needed me to be.

I felt this was especially true during times when people came to visit her. Coming from a large family, with many aunts, uncles and cousins, the hospital room sometimes felt claustrophobic. The endless questions and the painful answers (repeated visit after visit) were draining. While I understood that everyone who came to see us were there because they cared, there came a point when I just wished everyone would leave us alone. I just wanted to be alone with Sonia. I just wanted to shut down and do nothing but be with her.

Only she understood what I was going through.

Things People Say

Initially I had found it hugely beneficial to tell anyone and everyone what had happened. At the hospital I wanted to give every visitor that came to see us a blow by blow description of the events that had lead us there. I wanted to shock them out of their safe little world and show them the harsh reality of life. It sounds mean-spirited, but it felt right. I felt that people needed to know this stuff. How else could they fully appreciate what I had been through?

I think this reaction came about as a mechanism to stop them from talking, because I found people who visited us had an intrinsic need to say something but usually what came out of their mouth was more hurtful or naive than they obviously realised.

Whether they said it or not, I felt that people assumed that because the baby had not been full-term, that it somehow was not a "proper" baby. I made extra effort, especially in Jasmine's case (being twenty weeks) to ensure that people understood that she had been born alive. That she had reacted when I slid my finger up the sole of her tiny foot. That she had held my finger for the few minutes that she was alive.

I learnt early on that people meant well, but really had no idea what to say. I tried not to bristle at the misguided attempts they made at trying to console us.

"You're both still young. You can have other children."

I think that one got to me the most. I'm sure if they thought about it they would realise that no child can replace another. Your first-born will always be your first-born.

I can't tell you how close I was to sometimes responding to this remark by biting back, "Is any one of your children more important to you than the others? Even if I do have other children they'll never replace the ones I've lost!"

Both Sonia and I are the second eldest child in our families. When we lost Sophie it hit me that I had lost the equivalent of myself. The world had lost the equivalent of my wife. It was a very sobering thought and brought home the shear gravity of the potential life that had been lost.

"It wasn't meant to be" and "These things happen for a reason" are other comments that just seemed heartless. I found that people said these things because they themselves couldn't make sense of what had happened and felt that there had to be a rational reason for the baby to have died, but that we mere mortals just didn't have the knowledge to work it out.

"God works in mysterious ways" also fit into this category. "At least she's in heaven now" was another that really got to me. I am a religious person, but I just couldn't accept the fact that God was responsible for this monstrous injustice and therefore that somehow made it okay.

"Time heals all wounds" is rubbish. While things do tend to get somewhat easier with time, the death of your baby is not a wound that heals completely. It will always be there. Some days it will hurt more than others. It will weep and fester. It will diminish and sometimes stop bleeding. But it will never go away. Frankly, I wouldn't want it to.

Down the track people asked questions like, "When do you think you'll be back to normal?" Sorry, this is the new normal. I will never be the person I used to be. How could I be? Either learn to accept me for who I am, wounds and all, or don't. Because I cannot change who I am. I am always going to be a bereaved father. There is no escaping that. I am learning to live with that. Everyone else needs to get on board or step off.

My mother's aunty asked my wife, "What did you do?" as if she somehow had caused this to happen. I nearly fell of my chair when I heard this. I could not believe the heartlessness of such a question. As if my wife wasn't going through enough without someone casting aspersions on her. We both saw mum's aunty as a woman from a different time and place (a galaxy far, far away), when situations like this were dealt with quite differently, and so we didn't let it get us down or take it to heart.

In bygone eras, a mother usually didn't even get to see her baby after it had died. There was little or no support for grieving parents. The whole situation was almost swept under the carpet. Babies were often buried in unmarked graves. Sometimes they were anonymously buried with an adult stranger who had died in the hospital around the same time, with neither the baby's parents nor the deceased adult's family knowing the truth of the matter. Thankfully we have come a long way since those days. Infant death is no longer a totally taboo subject. Although, there is always room for improvement.

Most people (mother's aunties aside) mean well. Their comments are their best efforts at trying to say something comforting. One of my wife's friends actually approached me and said, "I don't know what to say to her". My response was to tell her that words weren't necessary. There are no words that can help make things better. Being there with her was enough. Actually, it was everything.

The Funeral

Coming home from the hospital was both relieving and distressing.

The familiar confines were comforting. Getting back to the safety of our home felt right.

However it also felt wrong. We were not supposed to be here under these circumstances. This had not been part of the plan. Coming home was supposed to be a joyful experience after you have had a baby.

While it was nice to be home, being there just made the reality of our situation all the more stark. This was it. This was the beginning of our new future. A future where our baby was dead. Being home minus our daughter made it real. It sunk in.

The house remained filled with family and relatives for some time. Coming from a big family meant we were never short of food or supplies. Everyone pitched in and helped with the everyday needs of living.

While her mother and sisters surrounded Sonia, I found myself in the company of my dad, uncle and a funeral director. I don't know who called him, but I understood the need for his presence and found myself once again with a task that required my input.

What did I want written on the tombstone? How did

A Bereaved Father

I spell my daughter's name? What date was she born on? What date did she die?

I have often heard the phrase, "No parent should have to bury their child". Truer words have never been spoken. Another is, "Life wasn't meant to be easy". Okay, but was it meant to be this hard?

For Jasmine's funeral only our immediate family attended. I remember arriving at the cemetery and discovering that my parents had given us the burial plot that they had bought for their final resting place. Jasmine would be buried next to my grandparents.

I was directed over to the funeral car, numbly following directions without any idea what I was supposed to do or what was supposed to happen. The back door opened and there lay a small white coffin. It was lifted out of the car and handed to me. I carried the surprisingly light coffin a short distance to the open grave. The rest is a blur. I remember Sonia, her mother, my mother, and others crying.

A year later, for Sophie's funeral, there were a lot more people in attendance. A lot more people had the chance to meet Sophie, as she had survived for three days in the hospital. Only our parents had seen Jasmine, who had only survived a few minutes. But Sophie got to meet our brothers and sisters, some aunts and uncles. I think to them Sophie was more real because of this. So her passing hit them harder than Jasmine's did.

Those same aunts and uncles, and other family and friends attended Sophie's funeral. Having had the experience of Jasmine's funeral, I felt more prepared the second time around. I knew what to expect. I knew what the coffin would look like, I knew I had to carry it, and how heavy it would be. It is a horrible thing to have experience at, but having done so made it somehow less confronting. Not so for those who had not attended Jasmine's funeral.

I remember the crying and sobbing was more evident at Sophie's funeral. The sorrow was more palpable. Yet strangely I felt stronger. Oddly, I also felt a sense of pride. I was bringing my daughters together, as Sophie would be buried in the same plot as her sister. These were my girls. My angels.

Going Back to Work

The days and weeks after your baby has died are strange. You look around at the world with new eyes.

"How can people just go about their regular business? Don't they know my baby has died?"

I looked at the world and wondered how I would ever fit back in. I was a changed person. I seriously doubted if I would ever be able to go back to my usual routine. How did I reconcile my previous place in the scheme of things with my new reality?

Grief theorists say that it is a masculine tendency to want to bury yourself in work as a way of exerting some control over things.

I did find solace in work related matters. I found tasks such as mowing the lawn, vacuuming the house, hanging out the washing therapeutic. They allowed my hands to be busy yet allowed my mind to wander where it needed to. I worked through things in my head.

I have worked in various jobs over the years. Big companies, small companies, and my own company (as the only employee). I have worked in places where I had my own private office, in others where I shared a room with a handful of co-workers, and I have also worked in an open-plan office where my cubicle was one of many.

Thankfully at the time when we lost both Jasmine and Sophie I was in a job that allowed me to work from home. It made it easier. I didn't feel any guilt about getting back to my work that I think I may have had if doing so meant leaving Sonia at home alone.

Working meant I had a program to follow. It helped make things seem sane again. There was some rationality back in my life. Work made sense.

One of the hardest things to figure out is just when the right time is to go back to work. When is too soon? How much time do you need off work? How much time can you afford not to work? All these factors come into play.

There are no right or wrong answers. I'm sure each case is different and the answers to these questions depend on what type of work you do, your position and responsibilities at work, and your financial situation.

How much time I dedicated to work, was however something I struggled with. On the one hand I sometimes didn't feel like working. I couldn't concentrate at times, and found it hard to focus on things that often felt trivial. On the other hand I felt a strong need to keep myself occupied. There were only so many household chores I could do around the house, so my work was often a refuge.

I questioned myself about whether by working I was

being useful and constructive, or whether I was just using it as an excuse to run away from my new reality and refusing to face the truth. And even though I was only in another room of the house, I wondered if I was somehow abandoning my wife, who hadn't yet returned to her work, and wouldn't for quite some time.

Depending on your job, you may not have had a choice about when to return to work. If you have been with an employer for twelve months of continuous service, then most Australian workplace agreements allow you to take twelve months unpaid paternal leave when your baby is born. However there does not seem to be much room in these workplace agreements for the father to take time off when a baby dies.

Parental leave allows both parents to remain off work for up to twelve months at the same time (unless you work for the same employer), which is usually set down to begin at a time around the "due date". Miscarriages and premature births don't adhere to any "due date", so it can be a difficult situation if your wife has a miscarriage or gives birth before she has taken her maternity leave. In these circumstances your wife is entitled to unpaid special maternity leave for as long as her doctor says it is necessary.[1] In our case, Sonia's employer was great and gave her as much time as she needed.

As the father, the workplace laws do not have a

---

[1] http://www.fairwork.gov.au/factsheets/FWO-Fact-sheet-Parental-leave-and-related-entitlements-and-the-NES.pdf

facility for unpaid special parental leave, however it may be possible for you to take annual leave or personal/carer's leave if it is available to you. I had no such qualms working from home for myself.

Whatever your situation, going back to work can be a stressful time. It is not only filled with emotional pitfalls and potholes, but it is also a time in your life where you are required to answer questions from colleagues, co-workers and clients.

Even though I work from home, I was still faced with phone calls, emails and instant messages from people who had no idea that my world had fallen apart. As is the case with many people I work with or for, my private life (and theirs) was not something discussed. We just spoke about work and nothing else. Therefore many people I dealt with did not even know my wife had been pregnant.

Those who did, but did not yet know what had happened, found out soon enough. How it affected them differed from person to person. What their reaction was towards me also differed greatly. Some were moved to write letters of support, others offered their condolences, one even wrote a lengthy poem.

But soon enough it was business as usual for 99.9% of them. They moved on with their work.

I know of bereaved fathers who regretted going back to work when they did. They found that they could not function in their particular role. Some had to take more time off, while others changed jobs completely.

I have heard of bosses who were very understanding, while others were extremely heartless. I have heard of colleagues who were a source of comfort, while others were uncomfortable being around someone who talked about their dead baby.

Yes, hindsight is 20/20 vision. It is easy to look back after the fact and think about what you would do differently in regards to going back to work. And even if you are reading this and have not yet returned to your regular job, no amount of advice will give you the correct answers. Only you can make those decisions.

Whatever you do or have done, when all is said and done, look back with the knowledge that you made the best decision you could at the time, based on the information you had at the time.

Birthdays, Christmas, Father's Day

As time goes by you will find yourself dreading certain future dates.

Festive occasions such as Christmas and Easter lose their gloss after your baby has died. All those hopes and dreams, the pictures in your head of how these days would look, the things you would do... they are now nothing but shattered bits of glass lying before you.

I am a big kid at heart. One of my favorite sayings is, "Growing old is mandatory. Growing up is optional." I always dreamed of the fun things I would do to make Christmas an occasion of wonderment for my children. I envisioned the stories I would tell, the make-believe games I would play with them surrounding Santa, waking up on Christmas morning to see them open their presents. None of this will happen for me now.

I do have nieces and nephews, and for them I continue to put up a Christmas tree and decorate the house. It's a discussion Sonia and I have every year. She would prefer I simply use the small 30cm ready-to-go Christmas tree we bought one year, rather than put up the 6-foot Christmas tree (which we bought when we were first married) that needs to be put together and decorated with lights, tinsel and hanging ornaments. She doesn't see the need, but for me it's something I have always done, ever since I was a child. I enjoy positioning the personalised shiny balls and angel decorations that have Jasmine and Sophie's names on them.

Easter and Christmas in my family have always equated to huge family gatherings. We have breakfast at my parent's place in the morning with mum and dad, my brother and sisters and their families (15 people all together); lunch at my in-law's house with Sonia's mum and dad, and her brother and sisters (a minimum of 12 people in total); and then dinner at my grandfather's house (my mum's father, the only living grandparent I have left), where all mum's side of the family gather (at the time of writing that could mean up to 40+ people). Needless to say, after we lost Jasmine and Sophie these gatherings became daunting occasions. It was extremely emotional and painful to see so many kids around, knowing that Jasmine and Sophie should have been amongst them. Watching each year as children, born the same year as our girls, grew older and bigger, wondering to myself how my daughter's would look in comparison.

No doubt you have your own customary practices and routines on these particular days. Be they big or small, involve extended family or not. Don't feel you have to keep up appearances. Do what works for you as a couple. The first year can be especially difficult. Subsequent years can get a little easier. You may decide to start your own new customs that include the child or children that are no longer with you. I know of couples that wrap up a present for their child and place it under the Christmas tree. Others purchase a present to give to a child via one of those Christmas charity appeals for underprivileged children often found in shopping centers. Do whatever works for you.

Without a doubt the hardest day you will have to endure in a calendar year is the anniversary of the day your child was born/died. For me those dates are July 11 (the day Sophie was born), July 14 (the day Sophie died), and July 24 (the day Jasmine was born and died). Obviously July isn't my favourite month of the year. Although it's a sweet and sour experience, as July 23 is also our wedding anniversary.

Sonia and I generally pick a day in July, around the middle of the month, to go visit the girls at the cemetery. We also go again around Christmas time. Our visits simply involve changing the flowers at the grave, cleaning away any dead leaves, and standing side-by-side for a few minutes of silence. We generally don't say anything... neither to each other nor to the girls. We just share some quiet time together, each lost in our own thoughts, but supporting each other nevertheless in the act of being there together.

I have heard of people who bake a cake and sing "Happy Birthday" at their baby's grave/headstone. I know of families that pack a picnic lunch, spread out a blanket and make an afternoon of it. Some bereaved parents go once a week or more, others just on special occasions, and some not at all. There is no right or wrong way. Once again it comes down to personal preference.

Father's Day is another day of the year that can be difficult to deal with. It may be different for fathers who have other children, but for me, having no living children, Father's Day can be a little tricky.

If you have other children, people will no doubt wish you a "Happy Father's Day", regardless whether or not they know you have lost a child. Whether it is a "happy" Father's Day is another matter altogether.

If, like me, you have no other children, you will notice a range of reactions (or non-reactions) from the people in your life. Some, like your work colleagues, will totally forget you are a father (or may not even think that a bereaved father is actually a father), and not say anything to you at all... even though they have just finished wishing the guy next to you a happy Father's Day. Family and friends who do remember your loss may struggle to know what to say. Obviously it's not a "happy" Father's Day for you, so while they want to acknowledge you on Father's Day, the usual greeting just doesn't fit. So some may flounder through a half-hearted "Happy Father's Day" greeting, while others, unable to come up with a better alternative, decide to say nothing at all.

Personally, while it's not a "happy" Father's Day for me, I would prefer people say "Happy Father's Day" than say nothing at all. At least that way I know that they acknowledge that I am indeed a father. It is the acknowledgment that counts more than anything else.

Depending on what kind of importance you and your family places on Father's Day it can be just like any other day, or it can be a more confronting experience. However, just like other special occasions and anniversaries, do what feels best for you. Skip over it or mark it however seems appropriate to you.

In my experience the thought of these approaching dates and special occasions are usually far worse than the actual days themselves. It is far too easy to look at the calendar and realise that a particular day is fast approaching and look upon this day with anxiety and fear. However, I think you will find that the build up in your heart and mind is much worse than the actual experience itself. It is a fear of the unknown. We worry about how we will feel and react on that day. We don't know what it will hold or how we will respond. We are not even sure if we will be able to face it at all. But in my experience those days come and go, and while they are far from a breeze, they are usually not as bad as we had anticipated. You look back on the day the next morning and realise that you not only survived, but you got through it relatively unscathed.

Having been through what we have been through already, was there really ever any doubt?

Family, Friends and Acquaintances

Family and friends can be a great source of comfort. It is worth remembering that they too have had a loss and are suffering on two different levels. In the case of your own parents, they are not only mourning the loss of a grandchild, but they are also hurting for you (their child) and the pain you are going through.

My mother was the first person I called on the day Jasmine was born. Even before dialing 000. The paramedics handed her the blanketed bundle that was our first-born daughter while they tended to Sonia. Mum carried Jasmine, no longer alive, in the second ambulance, while I traveled with Sonia in the other. I can only imagine what kind of experience that was for her.

At the hospital, my father and Sonia's parents joined my mother, as Jasmine was cleaned, measured and weighed. Nobody else from our families got to see her, except in the photos we took home with us.

Initially, in the days and weeks after, your family will mourn with you, and your situation will be the focus of everyone's lives. However, before too long their own lives and families once again take precedence and, for them, things return to normal. When this happens it is easy to feel left behind. You feel like everyone else has forgotten about your baby and are going on with their lives like nothing ever happened.

It's not true, they do remember. But unlike you and your wife, it is not the focus of their lives. Understanding this (and we all do on some level) does not make it any easier. You still feel alone. You still feel like the world has forgotten.

What I have learned is that family and friends are usually at a loss as to what comes next after the initial grieving period. They don't know what their role is or what they are supposed to do. They don't know whether you want them to talk about your baby, because they don't want to upset you. But by the same token they don't want you to think that they have forgotten them either. So they err on the side of keeping silent.

As the bereaved father, I look at it in the same manner as I see the "Happy Father's Day" comment, I would prefer they acknowledge my daughters by talking to me about them, rather than not say anything because they are worried they will upset me.

Yes, I probably will get emotional when I talk about them, but that's okay. Don't feel bad if I do get upset, because it is only natural for a father to feel sadness for their dead child. But any father will tell you that the thought of their dead child is far less painful to think about then the thought that the world might forget them. We want the world to remember them.

Men aren't usually the ones to broach emotional

subjects in the first place, so it can be a catch-22 situation. We want our baby to be remembered, but we are not always good at opening the topic ourselves. Some men are better at it than others.

Worrying that people do not want to hear about your dead baby can also be a difficult thing to get around. I sometimes worried that discussing my situation amongst "polite company" may not be appreciated. Death is a difficult topic at the best of times; the death of a baby isn't exactly a topic people are accustomed to. That is not to say that I was embarrassed by my story. Far from it. If anything I saw it as a badge of honour. It was more that I sometimes didn't feel that certain people were worthy of the story.

Often I would come across people I had not seen in a long time. Catching up with past acquaintances like old school friends or work colleagues would generally lead in to questions like, "Are you married? How many kids do you have?" Innocent enough questions. We have asked them ourselves a hundred times in the past. But in this new reality we find ourselves in, the "How many kids do you have?" question can be a tricky one to answer.

I found that my response to this question changed depending on the person asking and the situation we were in at the time. Think of it this way... Most of us ask, "How are you?" without really meaning it. We ask a person how they are without really wanting the warts-and-all answer. We simply expect them to reply with, "Fine thanks". Nobody really expects someone to reply to "How are you?" with a detailed list of medical ailments, mental complaints and personal relationship problems.

Similarly, if the person asking me, "How many kids do you have?" has asked me that question in the context of a quick "Hi/Bye" passing-in-the-street conversation, then my response will likely be a simple, "none". I will admit that I do feel guilty about doing so, but the reality of the situation necessitated a "get out quick" reply. Some people just didn't seem worth the effort. That sounds mean, but it's the truth. There are certain people and places that just are not receptive to the kind of explanation that is needed with an open and honest answer to that question.

Most times however I will answer with "We had two girls but they were both born too premature to survive. I have no other children." This tends to get one of two responses. "Oh, I'm so sorry!" followed by a change of topic. Or "Oh, I'm so sorry!" followed by a question wanting to know more.

I'm fine with either response. After all, if I had asked them "How many children do you have?" and let us say they replied with an answer of "Two", depending on who they are and what they mean to me, I might additionally ask, "How old are they? What are their names?" Alternatively, I might just leave it at their answer of "Two" and move on to talk about other things.

I'm happy to talk about my girls. I'm fine with giving people a basic story of when they were born, when they died, and what their names are. I also understand that some people are as disinterested in my children as I may be about theirs. That is just the way people are, depending on how well you know them.

Again, this may come across as cold, but as a bereaved father with no living children, I find it difficult to listen to other fathers talk about the escapades of their children. Their first tooth. Their first word spoken. What he/she did with their food this morning. All these things and others are moments I will never get to experience with my daughters. I don't begrudge them the joy their children bring them. It's just not something that is easy to listen to from where I'm standing.

I love children. I love being around them. Being a big kid at heart, I love spending time with my nieces and nephews. I love playing games with them, watching cartoons, telling stories. I have realised that as an uncle I can play an important role in their lives, which in turn enriches my life. It is not the same as being a father, but it is a role I enjoy and cherish. Besides, if they get too rowdy I can just hand them back to their parents.

Talking Helps

As a child, I was never very talkative. Throughout school and my teenage years I tended to be somewhat shy, preferring my own company to those of other people. I would spend hours in by bedroom reading, playing my guitar or listening to music. I had one or two good, close friends, rather than a large circle of friends.

While I was never a big talker, I was always confident within myself. I had no problem getting up to speak in front of people. I even fronted a music band as lead singer, and performed as an actor in front of audiences. It was the one-on-one conversations I wasn't too confident at.

Through my experiences with losing both Jasmine and Sophie, I found that I not only grew more confident, but that I actually enjoyed talking to people. It helped me immensely in my healing process.

Before Jasmine and Sophie I would have baulked at the idea of seeing a counselor or attending a support group. Guys don't tend to want to admit they need help. Going to see a "Shrink" holds almost as much fear for us as going to the Dentist.

I remember not being overly impressed with the hospital's counselor who we first met a few days after losing Jasmine. She was very personable and caring, but I just didn't feel like I got a lot out of it. When it was suggested to Sonia and I that we might like to attend a SIDS and Kids support group, I didn't exactly jump at the opportunity, but we agreed to go together. This was probably the best decision we ever made.

Attending the SIDS and Kids support group, which met on the first Wednesday of every month, was very rewarding. While the number of people who attended from month to month fluctuated, there tended to be anywhere from a half dozen to a dozen people every time. The groups were made up of mostly women, but I don't think I ever attended a meeting where there wasn't at least one other man.

I would encourage men to go along with their partners to a support group as it can give you an insight into her experience by hearing her talk in a group environment about things you might not have been aware of. I found that other women also found it helpful hearing from me, which in turn gave them an insight into their husband's grieving experience.

Being a member of these support groups helped me realise I wasn't alone. The other people in the group, while having different experiences, all shared a common bond. We were all bereaved parents. We all could relate to one another.

The support groups were the one place where I could tell my story, talk about the difficulties I was having, and look around the room and see nodding heads. These people understood where I was coming from. Instead of the blank (but caring) looks I would get from people who had never lost a child, in the group meetings I was faced with people who really knew what I was on about. They got it. They offered advice that came from experience. They shared their own experiences that shed light on topics I had been wondering about. They laughed and cried with me.

Sometimes it is easier to talk to someone you don't know, someone who does not have a preconceived idea of who you are and how you are supposed to act. I found it easier to open up to people who would not judge me based on our relationship or how they knew me. Your family and friends will often say what they think you want to hear, rather than what you actually need to hear. They are worried about hurting your feelings or dredging up sensitive topics they feel best left in the past.

Group discussions or one-on-one discussions with other bereaved parents or trained bereavement counselors can be a great way to deal with the stuff going on inside your head. It helped me immensely. You don't have to go regularly, just when you feel the need. Sonia and I went regularly for the first few months, and then only when we felt like it, such as July (the girls' anniversaries) and December (leading up to Christmas). Eventually we stopped going altogether.

There are no rules or formalities to the support groups we have attended. Initially everyone introduces themselves and gives a brief summary of the baby (or babies) that died, and that's it. From there it's an open floor. Talk as much or as little as you like. I have been to support groups where some people didn't talk at all, preferring instead to listen to what others had to say, learning from their experiences. With couples that attended, sometimes one spoke on behalf of the pair. Sometimes the husband would talk because the wife was too emotional. Sometimes the wife did all the talking because the husband simply preferred not to.

Some weeks I would have questions I wanted to ask other couples regarding how they had dealt with a certain issue. Other times I would just listen and interject where I felt I had something to add. All in all I would always walk out of the support group feeling like a load had been lifted off my shoulders.

While it was always sad to see a new couple attend the group for the first time, I felt better for them at the end of the hour-long meeting, as they seemed to have gained some strength from having shared their experience. I know that through these group meetings I no longer felt alone in the world. It helped to know that there were people who had been through a similar experience and survived.

So if going to a group meeting for you is akin to pulling teeth. Relax. They are nowhere near that bad. You might be surprised at what you get out of going. If nothing else, go along to support your wife. You might learn a thing or two about her that will help you, as a couple.

Remembering Them

Time waits for no man. Weeks become months, months become years, and life does go on, whether you feel like you want it to or not.

John Lennon said it best in his song "Beautiful Boy" when he wrote:

"Life is what happens to you while you're busy making other plans."

Life does go on, and the rest of the world seems to motor on despite how you feel or what you have lost. So it is important to remember your child (or children) in your own way.

For me, as a creative-type person, I poured my heart into writing a poem for each of my daughters. I also wrote, sang and recorded a song titled "Nobody Knows Who I Am" about how I was feeling alienated and apart from everything else. I also put music to a poem my wife had written (which I titled "Sonia's Lament"). [The lyrics to both these songs and my poems can be found at the end of this book].

On the stairwell of our house I painted a large picture of two cherubs (representing Jasmine and Sophie) reaching out to embrace each other.

In our backyard garden we placed a cherub birdbath and in front of it planted a Jasmine plant.

A Bereaved Father

There are many ways you can remember your child. Photos, artistic portraits (made professionally or created yourself), paintings, sketches. You can light candles, display a toy or figurine, plant a tree, or display a bunch of flowers.

I know of one father who has a small snow globe they bought for his son, on the base it reads 'special little boy'. Each morning, before he leaves for work, he greets his son and wishes him a good day, shakes the snow globe, places it back on the shelf, and walks out of the house. At night, he repeats the ritual and says goodnight to his son and tells him that he loves him. Little rituals like this can be your own personal way of ensuring your child is a regular part of your life.

Again, there is no right or wrong thing to do. Do as much or as little as suits you. No matter whether you can write, sing, or draw, each person has some way in which they like to remember their baby. It can be something momentous, or something simple. It can be for public display or for your own private viewing. It can be something physical you can hold, see or listen to. Or it can be something mental that you think or feel.

Here are some additional ideas that bereaved parents can do to memorialise their baby:

- Hold a memorial service.

- Make a public gesture (such as a donation) in your baby's name.

- Submit a poem to a newspaper or magazine (such as SIDS and Kids' "Connections" newsletter).

- Creating a memories box that includes photos, birth certificate, cards, clothes, baby blanket, etc...

- Put together a photo album.

- Wear a locket and put a picture of your baby in it.

- Commission a sketch or painting of your baby.

- Plant a tree or garden.

- Keep an angel statue or some other figurine in your home.

- Place a memorial plaque in your home or garden.

Marriage

You often hear people say that if a couple can get through the stress of planning their wedding that they can get through anything. I'm sure you will agree with me when I say that planning a wedding is nothing compared to the stress you feel when your baby dies.

You can't plan for something you never, not in your worst nightmares, dreamed could happen.

Who knew that "For better or for worse" meant this?

For me, the experience of Jasmine and Sophie's deaths brought Sonia and I closer together. We relied on each other for strength and support. I think we managed as well as we did because we were always open and honest with each other about how we were feeling and what we were going through. Attending the group meetings together helped us realise things about each other that we might not have been able to talk about if left to our own resources.

I found that Sonia needed validation from me. She needed to know that I still loved her and valued her. My reassurance to her that I loved her, no matter what, was something I did, and did often. I needed to let her know that I had married her because I loved her and wanted to spend the rest of my life with her. Whether or not we could have children was secondary. It wasn't the reason I had married her.

It was also essential that she understood that I did not blame her or hold her responsible for what had happened. It was just as much out of her control as it was mine. Further more, I needed to reassure her that she also should not attribute any blame upon herself. Nothing she did made this happen. There was nothing she could have done differently to create a different outcome.

When your baby dies it changes you as a person. It can also change you as a couple. Your roles in your relationship can change. Because men and women often grieve differently you may find that your roles and responsibilities in your home shift depending on how your method of coping with your grief differs from that of your wife.

Understanding that your wife may grieve differently to how you grieve is the key. If either tries to make the other conform to their way of grieving, it could lead to relationship difficulties.

I don't think a woman would appreciate her husband telling her that if she just gets dressed and puts on some make-up that she will feel better. Just as a man doesn't necessarily like being told that he never wants to talk about his dead baby when his wife wants to talk about them.

There are feminine and masculine methods of dealing with grief, both men and women can display both feminine and masculine grief traits, and will do so at different times.

In talking with other bereaved fathers I have found

that as husbands we shared similar feelings of wanting to protect our wife by not wanting to rock the boat. While we had our own thoughts and ideas on how we would like to remember our children, we were happy to go along with any suggestions our wife had on the matter.

Some might see that as laziness or apathy, but that's not the case. For me, I did the things that were important for me to do, like write poems and songs, but when it came to things we did as a couple, I was happy to concede to my wife's wishes, not because I didn't have any ideas of my own, but because I felt that her needs in these matters were more important than my own. I wanted to do whatever I could to make her feel better.

As the years go by, the opportunities to focus on our girls seem to be fewer and far between. For Sonia and I, the SIDS and Kids "Connections" newsletter gives us an opportunity to sit down and set aside some time for that very purpose. When a new "Connections" newsletter arrives in the mail we will pick a night during the week to turn off the TV, sit side-by-side on the sofa and read through the newsletter out loud. I'm usually the one doing the reading, as Sonia gets too emotional reading the letters and poems sent in by other bereaved parents. That's not to say that I don't get choked up or have tears in my eyes as I do so. It's hard not to be affected as you relate to the outpouring of emotion from people whose loss is so recent and raw.

When we were younger we simply thought we would get married and have kids. That's the plan for most of us. Plain and simple.

Sonia and I were married in 1994. We spent the first nine years of our life together trying to fall pregnant (both naturally and through IVF), only to have our first pregnancy end twenty weeks in in tragedy. A year later, it happened again. Add to that a subsequent miscarriage, and you find yourself looking at a couple that has been to Hell and back.

Thankfully we took that journey hand in hand, and continue to do so every day.

Subsequent Pregnancies and Other Children

I have often heard people say that they once believed that everyone would have something bad happen to them once in their life. Loss in some form is inevitable. The thing is, this belief comes with the understanding that once you have had that bad thing happen to you that you are then in the clear. You have had your bad thing happen, you are now done. You have fulfilled your quota.

After we lost Jasmine and then fell pregnant (naturally) with Sophie, I too thought that surely the same thing couldn't happen again. Lightning doesn't strike the same spot twice. I now know it can and does. Sometimes more than twice. I met a brave lady who has had seven miscarriages.

The loss of both Jasmine and Sophie, and the additional miscarriage, lead Sonia and I to decide not to try again. We had seen the best doctors and professors who dealt with high-risk pregnancies, and had dedicated most of our married life together towards trying to start a family. Physically Sonia was unlikely to carry a pregnancy to full-term. Mentally neither of us felt prepared to tempt fate again.

I was a mental wreck throughout Sonia's pregnancy with Sophie. When a third pregnancy ended with an early miscarriage, I couldn't bare the thought of another. Not for myself and especially not for Sonia's sake. Just the thought of it scared me. I couldn't do this anymore.

Sonia felt the same way. While it was mentally draining for me, it was both mentally and physically taking its toll on her.

We discussed adoption, but for me it had never been about just having children, it was about having our children, a life made up of the two of us.

My parents were both born in Lebanon, having migrated to Australia with their families when they were just children. As a first generation Australian, I had grown up as a redheaded, fair-skinned boy in a family made up of dark-haired, darker complexion people. I had received a recessive gene that popped up on my Dad's side of the family. His great grandmother had red hair, as did one of my first cousins. But nevertheless, people sometimes thought I was adopted. I had people call me the "Milkman's Son", which angered me from my own point of view and because of the light it portrayed my mother in.

I always felt proud when someone said I had my mother's eyes or that my voice sounded like my father's.

Families are always looking at a child as it grows up, comparing their baby photos to those of the parent's or aunties and uncles. We compare a child's looks to that of their parent's all the time.

Maybe it's selfish, but I had wanted to have our

baby. I wanted to be able to look at our child and say it had Sonia's eyes or mouth. I wanted that desperately.

We briefly considered surrogacy, but there were just so many logistical and legal loopholes that it was nothing more than a cursory consideration. We knew too well that pregnancies were not guaranteed outcomes. What if we selected a sister or cousin who was willing to be a surrogate mother for us, and something happened? What if the woman herself suffered some kind of complication while being pregnant with our child? What if that pregnancy failed and the baby died? How could we live with that? How much further stress would that add to the situation? It just seemed much too complicated for me to consider it. Oh, I know personally of people for whom it was a great success. But I just couldn't think of putting anyone in that position.

While I don't have any living children, I know of many fathers who have gone on to have successful pregnancies after the loss of a baby. While these additional children will never replace the one(s) that died, they are nevertheless a joy in their life.

While Jasmine was our first child, I know of many fathers who had older children living at home at the time their baby died.

Both these situations can have their own challenges.

Any subsequent pregnancy and child will obviously have challenges born out of the fear that something can go wrong, again, and that 'something' can be completely out of your control, or that it could occur despite all the preventative things you and your partner do to try and ensure a successful outcome.

The specific challenges you face may vary depending upon what caused the death of your baby and at what stage of your baby's life he or she died. For example, if your baby died during a premature birth, the fear of this happening again due to whatever physical or medical situation arose before may be a focal challenge, and the preventative measures such as pre-labour surgery and bed rest for your partner can present emotional, physical or even financial challenges if this means your partner has to stop working early in the pregnancy and you ordinarily rely on two incomes to support your family. Or, if your baby died due to cot death (SIDS), the pregnancy itself may not be the instinctive focal challenge, but rather an overwhelming worry about the baby after birth, when he or she is sleeping and a constant desire to keep checking on him or her recurs.

I think it is important to discuss with your partner what the specific concerns are that have come from the previous experience, to identify them together as clearly as you can, and to come up with ways together of how you want to manage or address those challenges as best you can as a team. That way you may be better prepared to face those challenges if and when they do present themselves, as opposed to dealing with them without having first considered ahead of time how they may impact upon your journey the next time around.

Something else to consider along with subsequent children, or previous, living children, is how you plan to explain to them that your baby died, and what it means to you, them and your family. How to do this is a totally subjective choice, and is up to you and your partner, however it is something that may inevitably come up with other children in the future if for instance they see photographs or hear conversations regarding your baby that has died. Children can have a way of discovering things on their own.

This can relate to how you may choose to remember or memorialise your baby and how you choose to explain (or not explain) to your other children what the death means and what has happened to your baby. As such, your particular beliefs or faith may impact on what you choose to do. It may be good to decide between the two of you on a consistent approach to this so that your children don't get confused, however this is something that really is a subjective choice, as, after all, you are obviously the parents of your children.

God, Faith and Religion

Whether you are a religious person or not, the death of your baby pulls at the very fabric of your faith in life.

Christian, Jewish, Muslim, Buddhist, Agnostic, Atheist... whatever you may be, there is nobody among us who believes that any parent should have to bury their child. Bad things aren't supposed to happen to good people.

As a Catholic, I have struggled and continue to struggle with how this all fits into what I believe as a Christian.

I am a regular churchgoer; I go to mass without fail every weekend. I pray every night before I go to sleep. But losing my daughters has lead to a lot of questions. Many remain unanswered to this day, and probably will until the day I die.

Why did God let this happen? Is it a test? Did He have a hand in it at all? Or do these things just happen? If God doesn't interfere (after all as a Christian I'm meant to believe He gave us Free Will), then why do we pray?

"Ask, and you will receive; seek, and you will find; knock, and the door will be opened to you. For everyone who asks will receive, and anyone who seeks will find, and the door will be opened to those who knock. Would any of you who are fathers give your son a stone when he asks for bread? Or would you give him a snake when he asks for a fish? As bad as you are, you know how to give good things to your children. How much more, then, will your Father in heaven give good things to those who ask him!" (Matthew 7:7-11)

If that is so, then why were our prayers for a happy and healthy baby not answered?

During the years when Sonia and I were trying to fall pregnant, I prayed each night, "God please help Sonia and I to fall pregnant". Then when we were pregnant I prayed for Sonia's pregnancy to be a "happy and healthy" one. I don't know if I ever thanked God for the fact that we were pregnant. And I don't know if I should have specified more details in my desire that the pregnancy go full-term and that the baby live. I kind of figured that went without saying. Nevertheless, I don't think that had I done so things would have turned out differently. I don't think God works that way. Regardless, I know that many of my family and relatives were also including Sonia and I in their prayers, so I think we were pretty well covered in that department.

I get irate when people tell me that when they drive into a parking area at the shops they say a quick prayer to God or a particular saint and lo and behold a parking space miraculously appears.

"Holy Mary full of grace, help me find a parking space."

Is one person finding the last car space more important to God than the next person behind them who misses out? Is a car space more important to God than the life of a baby?

It gets even more infuriating when you turn on the TV news and see a story about drug addict parents who leave their five children home alone in squalor for a week. You wonder why people, who don't want or care about children, can have them, but you and your wife, who want to bring up children in a loving, caring environment, can't? It doesn't seem fair or right.

I know in my heart that God doesn't make these things happen. And I also understand that were God to intervene in every dangerous or potentially upsetting situation that I would never learn or grow as a person. Just as our parents had to allow us to learn from our own mistakes, I understand that God allows me the room to grow and learn from the things that happen to me in my life, both good and bad. Understanding this doesn't make it any easier to live with though. It still hurts, it still feels unfair, and it still makes me angry.

For centuries Catholics were lead to believe that unbaptised babies did not go to Heaven, that they went to some place called "Limbo" instead. Even as a young boy I couldn't accept this. It seemed unlike the God I believed in for this to be true. In 2007 the Vatican announced that they had changed their stance on Limbo after a lengthy investigation and had decided that unbaptised babies do go to Heaven after all[2].

In researching this idea of Limbo I was aghast at some of the early church teachings I found. Supposedly, in the fourth century St. Augustine decided that unbaptised babies must be punished in the fire of hell, but only with the "mildest condemnation"[3]. Thomas Aquinas, eight hundred years later also thought that infant souls wouldn't go to heaven, but he was of the opinion that they wouldn't suffer in the afterlife, either (and they wouldn't even know what they were missing)[4].

Heavy stuff indeed. For those who behold themselves to the church's teachings, the change in the Vatican's views will be of great comfort. For me, I have always believed that my girls are in Heaven. I pray that we will be reunited there one day.

I know that not everyone is religious, and those that are might well be of different faiths and devote themselves by varying degrees. Whether you believe in an afterlife, or whether you believe that death is the end and there is nothing beyond, it is still hard to accept that your baby has died. It is hard to find a rhyme or reason for it. Whether you think of your baby as an angel in heaven or as a memory in your heart, their passing just doesn't fit in with the way things are "supposed to be".

---

[2] http://www.catholicnews.com/data/stories/cns/0702216.htm

[3] http://www.ccel.org/ccel/schaff/npnf105.x.iii.xxi.html

[4] http://www.ccel.org/ccel/schaff/hcc6.iii.xvi.x.html

I do believe in God. I do believe that my girls are together in heaven.

Afterword

Sonia sometimes asks me if I think about the girls every day. I do. They are in my prayers every night. Although, as the years go by, they don't necessarily enter my mind during the day, every day. They are never far from my thoughts, they will always be in my heart, but it is only natural that those who are no longer with us lose some focus in our everyday lives. We don't talk about them as much as we used to, but that doesn't mean we love them any less or don't wish they were with us.

I look at my future now, and compare it to the hopes and dreams I had before my girls were conceived. It is a far different future than I envisioned. There are no birthday parties, no bedtime stories, no kisses goodnight, no first day of school, no report cards or graduations, no driving lessons, no walking them down the aisle.

By the same token there will be no dirty nappies, no homework, no broken bones, no broken hearts, no worrisome boyfriends, no drug and alcohol concerns, no curfews missed.

Every cloud has a silver lining. You have to look for the positives in everything.

Sonia and I are very happily married. We are very much in love (perhaps more now than ever). We enjoy our life together. But our house will always be poorer for not having Jasmine and Sophie with us. Yet they are with us. In our hearts and in our minds. I will always be the father of two girls. I will always remember them.

I will always love them...

Appendix: Poems and Song Lyrics

My Little Flower - Jasmine

[For Jasmine Younis. Born/Died: July 24, 2003.]

I wish you'd met my little flower,
And felt her little touch;
Why, oh why did things turn sour?
We wanted her so much.

I'll never see my little flower,
I'll never watch her bloom;
She couldn't even stay one hour,
She left us all too soon.

I couldn't save my little flower,
Nothing anyone could do;
I didn't have a cape, no powers,
Felt helpless through and through.

Why can't I see my little flower?
Why do I feel so sad?
Please bring back my little flower,
I want to be her Dad.

Poem For Sophie

[For Sophie Jessica Younis. Born: July 11, 2004/Died:
July 14, 2004.]

Things all out of focus.
The world seems somehow tainted.
Everything in shades of gray.
Like God forgot to paint it.

Day is night and night is day.
They all just seem to blend.
Shattered dreams and broken hearts
that time will never mend.

Nothing seems to sound quite right.
Music's all out of tune.
It's all because you came too early...
and left us all too soon.

Another daughter I will miss,
another up in Heaven.
Dear Sophie say hello to your sister,
say hello to Jasmine.

Nobody Knows Who I Am

Lyrics by Steve Younis

1.   You'll be waiting a lifetime if you think
      somehow that I'm going to be the same as I
      was yesterday.

      Those days have gone by, circumstances
      have changed, why can't you see me for
      who I am today?

Chorus: Nobody knows who I am.

      They expect me to be the person I used to be

      but I'm not that person anymore. I can't go
      back to who I was before.

2.   I've been through some changes, sorrow all
      through the pages of my life, but what's
      been done can't be undone.

      There's so much I've had to bear, I know
      that you really care, but can you learn to
      love who I've become?

Chorus: Nobody knows who I am.

      They expect me to be the person I used to be

      but I'm not that person anymore. I can't go
      back to who I was before.

3.　　　Some days I'll be feeling down, on others I
　　　　will play the clown.

　　　　God knows what kind of day it's gonna be.

　　　　But wouldn't it be a shame if we never
　　　　spoke their names?

　　　　I may still cry but that's okay with me.

Chorus: Nobody knows who I am.

　　　　They expect me to be the person I used to be

　　　　but I'm not that person anymore. I can't go
　　　　back to who I was before.

　　　　Do you know who I am?

Sonia's Lament

Lyrics by Sonia Younis

1. You're always on my mind, no matter what
    I do,
    I just wish I could see you and be with you.

2. I know that life it goes on, believe me so it
    should,
    But I wish that you could be here, back for
    good.

Chorus: Life goes on and time it heals,
        Wish people weren't afraid of how I feel.
        What life deals us we just don't know,
        What tomorrow may bring, God only
        knows.

3. People seem to forget just how I feel.
    I wish they would acknowledge that this is
    all real.

4. They seem to shut it all out to calm their
    own fears.
    They don't know what to do when they see
    me in tears.

Chorus: Life goes on and time it heals,
        Wish people weren't afraid of how I feel.
        What life deals us we just don't know,
        What tomorrow may bring, God only
        knows.

5. I think of you both often to keep me strong.
    I know you wouldn't want me to hurt too
    long.

6. The thought of you my Angels makes me
    stronger each day.
    Forever in my heart you'll always stay.

Chorus: Life goes on and time it heals,
        Wish people weren't afraid of how I feel.
        What life deals us we just don't know,
        What tomorrow may bring, God only
        knows.

Acknowledgements

Deciding to write a book such as this isn't exactly an easy thing to do. It came about through much encouragement and support from a range of people.

First and foremost I could not have written this book without the love and support of my wife, Sonia. She is an inspiration to me every day of my life.

A big thank you to the staff at SIDS and Kids for their support and enthusiasm. A special thank you to both Margaret McSpedden and Helen Wilkinson for their feedback and assistance.

Thanks also to Kaan McGregor for his invaluable assistance as a fellow bereaved father.

Many thanks to Neal Bailey for inspiring me as a writer, a true friend, and my right hand man.

Thank you to my family, mum (Anne), dad (Joe), Joanne, Carolyn, Jeffrey, Joe, Ray, Therese, Emma, April, Anne, Christian, and Gabrielle. To Sonia's family, her mum (Julie), dad (Samir), Lisa, Helen, Laura (RIP), David, Edward, Teresa, Armani, Jacque, and Tiarna.

To fellow bereaved parents I've met over the years, thank you for sharing your stories and experiences.

Last, but by no means least, thank you to my daughters Jasmine and Sophie for coming into my life, if only so briefly.